LOVE POEMS FROM THE HEBREW

LOVE POEMS
FROM THE
HEBREW

EDITED BY DAVID C. GROSS

Illustrated by Shraga Weil

DOUBLEDAY & COMPANY, INC.
Garden City, New York
1976

DESIGNED BY LAURENCE ALEXANDER

Library of Congress Cataloging in Publication Data
Main entry under title:

Love poems from the Hebrew.

Includes index.
1. Love poetry, Hebrew—Translations into English.
2. Love poetry, English—Translations from Hebrew.
I. Gross, David C., 1923–
PJ5059.E3L6   892.4'1'008
ISBN 0-385-11136-3
Library of Congress Catalog Card Number 75-45224
Copyright © 1976 by David C. Gross

ACKNOWLEDGMENTS

The editor and publisher express their appreciation to the following for permission to include the material indicated:

JEWISH PUBLICATION SOCIETY OF AMERICA for "A Woman of Valour" and "Too Wonderful" (Book of Proverbs); "Set Me As a Seal upon Thy Heart," "Let Him Kiss Me," "Hark! My Beloved," "On My Bed I Sought Him," "I Am My Beloved's," "Behold Thou Art Fair," "I Sleep but My Heart Waketh," "Return, Return O Shulammite" (Song of Songs) from The Holy Scriptures; "The Fair Maiden," "To the Bridegroom," "Ophra," "Parting," "The Dove" from Selected Poems of Judah Halevi, translated by Nina Salaman; "Awake, My Fair," "Marriage Song," "Far Sweeter Than Honey" from Book of Delight and Other Papers, by Israel Abrahams; "Ode to a Bridegroom" from Jewish Life in the Middle Ages, by Israel Abrahams; "Rejoice, O Youth, in the Lovely Hind," "Beautiful Is the Loved One," "When She Plays upon the Harp or Lute," "Those Beauteous Maids," "With Hopeless Love," "Strange Love," "Elegy," "My Love Is Like a Myrtle" from Selected Poems of Moses Ibn Ezra, translated by Solomon Solis-Cohen; all reprinted by permission of The Jewish Publication Society of America.

JEWISH QUARTERLY REVIEW for Samuele Romanelli's "Love," translated by A. B. Rhine, copyright 1911; reprinted by permission of the Jewish Quarterly Review.

SCHOCKEN BOOKS, INC., and VICTOR GOLLANCZ, LTD. for "Father's Gone Far, Far Away," "The Marriage Jester's Song," "Wedding Gifts," from S. Y. Agnon's The Bridal Canopy, translated by I. M. Lask, Copyright © 1967 by Schocken Books, Inc.; reprinted by permission of Schocken Books, Inc.

BRANDEN PRESS, INC. for "Her Eyes," "A Star There Fell," "Come, Let Us Exalt in Love's Passion," "There Was a King in Judah," from Titans of Hebrew Verse by Harry H. Fein. Copyright 1936 by Bruce Humphries, Inc.; reprinted by permission of Branden Press, Inc.

DAVID HIGHAM ASSOCIATES for "A Secret Kept," "The Apple," from *The Jewish Poets of Spain* by David Goldstein; reprinted by permission of David Higham Associates.

A. S. BARNES & COMPANY, INC., for "The Golden Peacock" by Chaim Bialik from *The Golden Peacock*; reprinted by permission of A. S. Barnes & Company, Inc.

UNIVERSITY OF CALIFORNIA PRESS for "Tirzah" and "Afternoon Light" from *Modern Hebrew Poetry*, edited and translated by Ruth Finer Mintz. Copyright © 1966 by The Regents of the University of California; reprinted by permission of the University of California Press.

ABELARD-SCHUMAN, INC., for "Man and Wife," "Neither Daily Neither Nightly," "The Love of Thérèse Du Meun," from *Anthology of Modern Hebrew Poetry*, edited and translated by Abraham Birman. Copyright © 1968 by Abraham Birman with permission of Abelard-Schuman.

EDITH SAMUEL for Chaim Nachman Bialik's "My Garden" (published by Histadruth Ivrith), "On a Hill" (published by *New Palestine*), "Shelter Me Beneath Your Pinion" (published by Union of American Hebrew Congregations), all translated by Maurice Samuel; reprinted by permission of Edith Samuel.

HISTADRUTH IVRITH OF AMERICA for "One Summer Evening," "Whence and Whither," "How Like Eyes" from *Selected Poems of Chaim Nachman Bialik*; reprinted by permission of Histadruth Ivrith of America.

SCHOCKEN BOOKS, INC., and VALLENTINE, MITCHELL & CO., LTD., for "Loneliness" from *Hannah Senesh: Her Life and Diary*. Copyright © 1966 by Hakibbutz Hameuchad Publishing House, Ltd. English edition copyright © 1971 by Nigel Marsh; reprinted by permission of Schocken Books., Inc., and Vallentine, Mitchell & Co., Ltd.

JOSEPH LEFTWICH for "One, Two, Three," translated by Joseph Leftwich in *Joseph Leftwich*, copyright 1939 by Sci-Art Publishers; reprinted by permission of Joseph Leftwich.

ACUM, LTD., for Yaacov Fichman's "Eve"; Rachel's "Michal" and "His Wife"; Yocheved Bat-Miriam's "If He Returns" and "Parting"; Nathan Alterman's "The Maiden" and "Song of the Wife"; I. Z. Rimon's "For a Girl's Tresses" and "I Have Learned to Mould"; S. Tchernikhovsky's "With This Ring I Thee Charm"; Yaacov Steinberg's "At Night"; David Fogel's "On My Pale Couch, My Body" and "If Night Nears Your Window"; Avraham Ben-Yitzhak's "Kingdom"; U. Z. Greenberg's "Like a Woman" from *Anthology of Modern Hebrew Poetry*, Volumes 1 and 2, published by the Institute for Translation of Hebrew Literature; reprinted by permission of Acum, Ltd.

In addition, the following poems have been taken from works currently in the public domain:

"Love Song," "Within My Heart" by Al-Harizi; "Love Song" by Halevi; and "Three Love Poems: 'He Cometh,' 'The Mirror,' and 'My Sweetheart's Dainty Lips,' " from *Collected Works of Emma Lazarus*, Volume II; copyright 1888 by Houghton Mifflin.

"Winged Its Way to Me Her Letter," from *Anthology of Poem Translations from Hebrew and Yiddish*; copyright 1930 by City Printing Works, Capetown, South Africa.

"Love Songs: 'The Splendor of Thine Eyes,' 'The Hot Flame of My Grief,' and 'Why Should I Grieve?',." from *When Love Passed By and Other Verses*; copyright 1939 by Rosenbach & Company, Philadelphia, Pennsylvania.

"Strange Matrimony," "A Husband's Complaint," "Happiness Amidst Troubles," "The Elusive Maid," and "The Unhappy Lover," from *Hebrew Humor*; copyright 1905 by Luzac & Company, London, England.

For Esther,
a woman of valour

PREFACE

John Milton said that good poetry should be "simple, sensuous, and passionate."

The Hebrew language, one of the oldest tongues known to man, is remarkably well suited to poetic expression: it is pithy, sparing of adjectives and adverbs, dependent primarily on nouns and verbs.

In biblical poetry, in particular, the lines are short and direct, depending on action, imagery, vigorousness, and simplicity to convey a mood.

Poets have been writing in Hebrew from the days of the Bible right down to the moderns in Israel today. A substantial part of the poetry created in Hebrew is religious and philosophical, reflecting the tribulations of the Jews, especially in the past two thousand years of exile and wandering.

But the theme of love remained vivid through the centuries of Jewish life. "Love is as strong as death," the Song of Songs tells us, which has elicited a Yiddish proverb: "Love tastes sweet, but only with bread."

Although the study of Hebrew has grown substantially in the United States, notably in the past quarter of a century, the ancient language of the Bible has never achieved the popularity of the Romance languages— despite the fact that up until the late eighteenth century, the study of Hebrew was a required course at Harvard and Yale, and was also taught at Princeton, Dartmouth, Brown and Columbia universities. In early New England, commencement exercises included addresses delivered in Hebrew.

I hope that this volume of love poems from the Hebrew language, spanning several millennia, will add joy and understanding—indeed, love—to all of its readers.

D. C. G.

LOVE POEMS FROM THE HEBREW

SET ME AS A SEAL UPON THY HEART

Set me as a seal upon thy heart,
As a seal upon thine arm;
For love is strong as death,
Jealousy is as cruel as the grave;
The flashes thereof are flashes of fire,
A very flame of the Lord.
Many waters cannot quench love,
Neither can the floods drown it;
If a man would give all the substance of his house for love,
He would utterly be contemned.

SONG OF SONGS 8:6–7

MAN AND WIFE

I wed you not with overwhelming lyre,
You won me by assurance deep and calm.
Our love-song was enhanced by wisdom's psalm,
You gave me all the light and hid the fire.

My soul was snugly sheltered in your palm
From straying wild, from deviation's briar;
And when despair would tempt me to retire,
Your tact and taste endowed me their balm.

How good to lean my head against your breast,
The warp of sorrow and the woof of joy
To weave around your heart in peace and rest.

With me you are—who will my lot destroy?
With you I am—sleep on, beloved name.
I guard your altar, keep the sacred flame.

SHIN SHALOM
(*Translated by Abraham Birman*)

KINGDOM

The daylight flickers on my crown,
Whose gold burdens my forehead,
The edges of my robe wash over the marble staircase,
The sea moans its fine evening grief.

Night's daughter, come quietly,
Sit at my feet on marble whiteness.
Let the wind lift your hair,
Such black hair.
The waters are rising:
Stay quiet
Till I tell you: Get up and sing.

AVRAHAM BEN-YITZHAK
(*Translated by Arthur Jacobs*)

AT NIGHT

My love I whispered, by your house at night:
You bent your head, your head of curly hair.
I in parables sheathed my delight
And lightly asked love's heavy riddle there.

Then your veil suddenly rustled: you seemed to wait.
Your eyelids trembled a little, as you faced me.
You were like a fish rising towards the bait.
The rustle of secrets moves with it through the sea.

YAACOV STEINBERG
(*Translated by Dom Moraes*)

PARTING

And dawn shall trail after me to the shore,
Like a child to play with shells:
Singing like a hope, shining like a tear,
Silent, the echo of what will befall.

On chill and sun he will describe his height
In a tall wide script: he shall not claim
Any remembrance of my form in flight,
My name, my humble other name.

My name which went singing for happiness,
For many griefs, and times I went astray.
With and above it, like a faltering promise
Stepped my great day.

A bit of it—like a scent, an echo—
I contained in the blue vase,
In the Chinese drawing made long ago,
Looking for its butterfly, its stalk of grass.

And a few books, not many, which looked out
At their moon leaving the river, on its way.
It taught a warm and festive solitude
And the sharp lustre of the faraway.

When the parting suddenly flings wide forever
The unknown distance, in a little while,
I'll remember everything by name, by the quiver
Of their wise and bashful smile.

I shall put my dead face on with a silence free
Of joy and of pain evermore,
And dawn will trail like a child after me
To play with shells on the shore.

YOCHEVED BAT-MIRIAM
(*Translated by Dom Moraes*)

MICHAL

And Michal, Saul's daughter, loved David—and she despised him in her heart.

> Though years divide, we're sisters yet;
> Your vineyard stands though weeds invade;
> Still tinkle anklet, amulet;
> Your red silk garment does not fade.
>
> By a small window still you stand,
> Proud, but a death within your eyes.
> My sister, I can understand—
> Whom also love whom I despise.

RACHEL
(*Translated by Robert Friend*)

TOO WONDERFUL

There are three things that are too wonderful for me,
Yea, four which I know not:
The way of an eagle in the air;
The way of a serpent upon the rock;
The way of a ship in the midst of the sea;
And the way of a man with a young woman.

PROVERBS 30:18–19

WITH THIS RING I THEE CHARM

With this ring I thee charm in the rite
Of the butterfly born to its world,
To its life of one day, the bridal night
Of one hour amid colored wings.
With this ring I thee charm in the plight
Of choirs of mosquitoes that dance
In the forest clearing, in the light
Of their mute song of noon's fiery romance.

With this ring I thee charm in the rite
Of the rustling tree and the plants
Fluttering in the breeze, that recite
In the tongue of aromas and speak only scents.
With this ring I thee charm in the ways
Of that great yearning that sings,
The great yearning, so silent always,
That blossoms again every year, every spring.

With this ring I thee charm in the rite
Of the bellowing deer that broods,
In longing for a mate, at twilight,
With glowing horns at the edge of the woods.
With this ring I thee charm with the power
Of all the might in animal essence,
Of worlds once destroyed and reborn in the roar
Of all the thousands of tribes of existence.

With this ring I thee charm, in the deep
Secret of all the poems of man and his song,
Of his magician's words, of the glories that sleep
In the mysteries of his faith, hidden so long
In the guess and the stress of each human heart,
In the source of his dance and the base of his art.
Bewitched, now be still—and never depart—
I thee charm thee forever . . . till death do us part . . .

SAUL TCHERNIKHOVSKY

(Translated by Richard Flantz)

LET HIM KISS ME

Let him kiss me with the kisses of his mouth—
For thy love is better than wine.
Thine ointments have a goodly fragrance;
Thy name is as ointment poured forth;
Therefore do the maidens love thee.
Draw me, we will run after thee;
The king hath brought me into his chambers;
We will be glad and rejoice in thee,
We will find thy love more fragrant than wine!
Sincerely do they love thee.

'I am black, but comely,
O ye daughters of Jerusalem,
As the tents of Kedar,
As the curtains of Solomon.
Look not upon me that I am swarthy,
That the sun hath tanned me;
My mother's sons were incensed against me,
They made me keeper of the vineyards;
But mine own vineyard have I not kept.'
Tell me, O thou whom my soul loveth,
Where thou feedest, where thou makest thy flock to rest at noon;
For why should I be as one that veileth herself
Beside the flocks of thy companions?
If thou knowest not, O thou fairest among women,
Go thy way forth by the footsteps of the flock
And feed thy kids, beside the shepherds' tents.
I have compared thee, O my love,
To a steed in Pharaoh's chariots.
Thy cheeks are comely with circlets,
Thy neck with beads.
We will make thee circlets of gold
With studs of silver.

While the king sat at his table,
My spikenard sent forth its fragrance.
My beloved is unto me as a bag of myrrh,
That lieth between my breasts.
My beloved is unto me as a cluster of henna
In the vineyards of En-gedi.

SONG OF SONGS 1:2–12

AWAKENING

Please pass your hands across my lips.
I'm not accustomed to this light.

Batlike our love in flight bangs round through dark.
It does not miss its mark: and your face shapes
My hands for me. What shall I learn in light?
Quick, pass your hand across me.

Your childhood (what's the time?) slept in my arms.
It's ten o'clock between the sea and night:
Midnight between us: seven between the blinds—
Oh no, I'm not accustomed to this light.

Which comes to make cold slits of both my eyes,
Opening like gunsights. On these scales I weigh
My blind eyes, and the terror of your clay.
Quick, pass your hand through me.

Face to face, I'll have no face, perhaps.
Perhaps I'll stay quiet, or perhaps I'll talk.
Please pass your hand across my lips.
I'm not accustomed to this light.

T. CARMI
(*Translated by Dom Moraes*)

ON MY PALE COUCH, MY BODY

On my pale couch, my body
In nakedness shines silently
Like white fire.

And the night of my hair,
A dark waterfall, floats free
To the weft of the rug.

Come, my lover.
Virgin, my beauty forever
Burns for the blue of your eyes.

Come . . .

It deepens, the red of my walls.

And the dusk, solitary,
Nears my couch,
And spreads a black dress
Over me.

And the two glimmering streams
Of my feet
I shall no longer see.
I cry, it is dark . . .

DAVID FOGEL
(*Translated by Dom Moraes*)

PARTING

If parting be decreed for the two of us,
Stand yet a little while I gaze upon thy face . . .

By the life of love, remember the days of thy longing,
As I remember the nights of thy delight.
As thine image passeth into my dreams,
So let me pass, I entreat thee, into thy dreams,
Between me and thee roar the waves of a sea of tears
And I cannot pass over unto thee.
But O, if thy steps should draw nigh to cross—
Then would its waters be divided at the touch of thy foot.
Would that after my death unto mine ears should come
The sound of the golden bells upon thy skirts!
Or shouldst thou be asking how farest thy beloved, I from the depths of
    the tomb
Would ask of thy love and thy welfare.
Verily, to the shedding of mine heart's blood
There be two witnesses, thy cheeks and thy lips.
How sayeth thou it is not true, since these be my witnesses
For my blood, and that thine hands have shed it?
Why desirest thou my death, whilst I but desire
To add years unto the years of thy life?
Though thou dost rob my slumber in the night of my longing,
Would I not give the sleep of mine eyes unto thy eyelids? . . .
Yea, between the bitter and the sweet standeth my heart—
The gall of parting, and the honey of thy kisses.
After thy words have beaten out my heart into thin plates,
Thine hands have cut it into shreds.
It is the likeness of rubies over pearls
What time I behold thy lips over thy teeth.
The sun is on thy face and thou spreadest out the night.
Over his radiance with the clouds of thy locks.
Fine silk and broidered work are the covering of thy body,
But grace and beauty are the covering of thine eyes.

The adornment of maidens is the work of human hands,
But thou—majesty and sweetness are thine adornment . . .
In the field of the daughters of delight, the sheaves of love
Make obeisance unto thy sheaf . . .
I cannot hear thy voice, but I hear
Upon the secret places of my heart, the sound of thy steps
On the day when thou wilt revive
The victims whom love for thee hath slain—on the day when thy dead
    shall live anew,
Then turn again to my soul to restore it to my body; for on the day
Of thy departure, when thou wentest forth, it went out after thee.

JUDAH HALEVI
(*Translated by Nina Salaman*)

LIKE A WOMAN

Like a woman who knows that her body entices me,
God taunts me, Flee if you can! But I can't flee,
For when I turn away from him, angry and heartsick,
With a vow on my lips like a burning coal:
I will not see him again—

I can't do it,
        I turn back
And knock on his door,
Tortured with longing

As though he had sent me a love letter.

URI ZVI GREENBERG
(*Translated by Robert Mezey and Ben Zion Gold*)

THE APPLE

You have captured me with your charm, my lady;
You have enslaved me brutally in your prison.
From the very day that we had to part
I have found no likeness to your beauty.
I console myself with a rosy apple,
Whose scent is like the myrrh of your nose and your lips,
Its shape like your breast, and its color
Like the hue which is seen on your cheeks.

JUDAH HALEVI
(*Translated by David Goldstein*)

A SECRET KEPT

The girl brought me into the house of love.
She was as pure and perfect as Abigail.
When she took off her veil she revealed a form
That put to shame the beauty of Esther.
Her light shone in the darkness, made everything tremble.
The hills started to dance like rams.
I thought: "Now our secrets are discovered."
But she stretched out her hand like a woman of strength
And enveloped me with her jet-black hair.
So the day was immediately turned into night.

JUDAH AL-HARIZI
(*Translated by David Goldstein*)

HOW LIKE EYES

"How like eyes they peep and sparkle
In the sky, the stars, tonight!"
Eyes they are, bright eyes of Cherubs
Who behold us from the height.

"Moonlight falling all around us,
Silver threads that lace the stream."
Brighter, softer, more entrancing,
Love, your loosened ringlets gleam.

"Clouds I see like snow-white marble,
Moonlit fragments, how they shine!"
Whiter, purer than those cloudlets
Are your thoughts which I divine.

"Diamond-like, the heavy dewdrops
Sparkle where the moonbeams fall."
Turn your eyes on me and show me
Jewels clearer than they all!

"Music of a fountain flowing,
Incense wafted from the hills."
Airs of Eden, sweet, your breathing;
In your voice are flutes and rills.

"Hark! the nightingale, peerless,
Chief of all the feathered throng . . ."
Night is fleet, to me be gracious!
Is not love the soul of song?

"Can this night not last for ever?
Can we keep it, can we hold? . . ."
Foolish child, this very question
As the universe is old!

CHAIM NACHMAN BIALIK
(*Translated by Helena Frank*)

HARK! MY BELOVED

Hark! my beloved! behold, he cometh,
Leaping upon the mountains, skipping upon the hills.
My beloved is like a gazelle or a young hart;
Behold, he standeth behind our wall,
He looketh in through the windows,
He peereth through the lattice.
My beloved spoke, and said unto me:
"Rise up, my love, my fair one, and come away.
For, lo, the winter is past,
The rain is over and gone;
The flowers appear on the earth;
The time of singing is come,
And the voice of the turtle is heard in our land;
The fig-tree putteth forth her green figs,
And the vines in blossom give forth their fragrance.
Arise, my love, my fair one, and come away.

SONG OF SONGS 2:8–13

THE UNHAPPY LOVER

O lovely maiden, thou hast drawn my heart
To thee, as though by some magician's art,
Yet though my love is like a glowing flame,
Thy coldness brings me but to scorn and shame.
Mind, if I perish through thy chill disdain,
The folks will say, "Here's one by woman slain."

JUDAH AL-HARIZI
(*Translated by J. Chotzner*)

Then the jester rose on his chair, each one brought him his wedding present, and he proclaimed it in rhyme and rhythm:

The magnate renowned, sire of the bride,
With his modest spouse, his crown and pride,
Shprintsa Pessil and Simeon Nathan,
Present to the bride and bridegroom one
Pair of candlesticks silver pure,
May their star shine bright and their star be sure,
While I the jester, Reb Joel hight,
Sing sweet song till Messiah's in sight
To honor thee bridegroom, and thee O bride
As the sun and the moon so clear and bright,
And all who can sing will sing and cheer
Till the end of a hundred and twenty year.

And the worthy uncle of the bride,
(Her uncle on the mother's side),
Gives them a current bill and leal,
Written and stamped with the duke's big seal.
Let my love to his garden to eat his fruits
And the Lord send him the blessing he boots.

The worthy kinsman tried and true,
Presenteth a wooden mortar and trough
For matzot, as Passover draweth near,
So sure may Redemption come to us here
When we'll eat of the offerings, the special and the plain,
And sing thanks to the Lord again and again.

> The honored Reb Elkanay, sterling as a guineay, gives as his gift—a silver wine cup and spice box for spices to be whiffed, one for hallowing the Sabbath on Friday night, and one for the ending of the Sabbath tide; upright let him walk in the Lord God's light, being saved from disease and blight and shielded always, to the very end of days.

Now what is the worthy gift of the fine and wealthy aunt? A copper laver as well as a mortar shows she regards her niece with favor, just as she oughter.

Last but not least that leader of Israel from belly and birth,
The princely Reb Israel Solomon, ruler over synagogue hearth,
Who reared the bridegroom as though he were an only son,
And took him and set him in a resting place all his own,
Delivering his soul from hunger and cold,
Feeding him, clothing him in fine array
And giving him dainties day after day,
Now offers him the scepter of gold,
Presenting him the four-volume Turim with every comment
And margins full broad for what he holds is meant,
O bridegroom, awaken, bestir thee, awaken, arise,
Show those margins thou'rt learned in Torah and wise;
Buckle thy learning upon thee and straight
Up and attack with thy quill; 'tis their fate.

The jester still stood on the chair looking this way and that and saying, What's the name of that fellow there, who hasn't given any present yet? And all those who had reckoned on getting away without any gifts trembled for fear of the jester's rhymes, and gave a coin which the jester would raise on high before the bride, saying in rhyme and rhythm:

This here coin, desired bride,
Has the face of the king on one side,
Let the Face of the King before thee be
And kingly rabbis be born of thee.

S. Y. AGNON
(*Translated by I. M. Lask*)

HER EYES

In the woodland I was roaming
　　When I first descried her;
She was saunt'ring 'mid the lotus,
　　And I slyly eyed her.

Ling'ring sunrays slowly dying
　　'Mong the leaves were beaming;
Discs of light like golden dinars
　　Through the shades were gleaming.

Lone she walked, her arms lay folded
　　On her bosom swaying;
Up and down the reddish light-discs
　　On her face were playing.

From her count'nance fell the light-discs
　　To the ground and stayed there;
Two resplendent rays fell also
　　On her eyes and played there.

Fell and played there—straightway stopped she,
　　Stood, nor word nor motion;
Glowed her eyes like two coals burning
　　In a flaming ocean.

Stared the maid, her eyes were burning—
　　God in heaven, savior!
Tell me what these eyes demanded . . .
　　Strange was their behavior.

Serpents two, oh, two black vipers
　　Forward saw I drawing;
From her eyes my heart they entered,
　　Hissing, biting, gnawing;

Biting, burning, venom pouring,
  Nigh their flames consumed me.
God, my God, destroy this demon!
  Lilith snared and doomed me.

On she went, her footsteps vanished,
  Woodland to me leaving;
But her eyes for aye pursue me,
  Aye, without retrieving!

CHAIM NACHMAN BIALIK
(*Translated by Harry H. Fein*)

THE GOLDEN PEACOCK

The golden peacock flies away.
Where are you flying, pretty bird?
I fly across the sea.
Please ask my love to write a word,
To write a word to me!
I know your love, and I shall bring
A letter back, to say,
With a thousand kisses, that for spring
He plans the wedding day.

CHAIM NACHMAN BIALIK
(*Translated by Joseph Leftwich*)

ON MY BED I SOUGHT HIM

By night on my bed I sought him whom my soul loveth;
I sought him, but I found him not.
"I will rise now, and go about the city,
In the streets and in the broad ways,
I will seek him whom my soul loveth."
I sought him, but I found him not.
The watchmen that go about the city found me;
"Saw ye whom my soul loveth?"
Scarce had I passed from them,
When I found him whom my soul loveth:
I held him, and would not let him go,
Until I had brought him into my mother's house,
And into the chamber of her that conceived me.
"I adjure you, O daughters of Jerusalem,
By the gazelles, and by the hinds of the field,
That ye awaken not, nor stir up love,
Until it please."

SONG OF SONGS 3:1–5

THE FAIR MAIDEN

The night when the fair maiden revealed the likeness of her form to me,
The warmth of her cheeks, the veil of her hair,
Golden like a topaz, covering
A brow of smoothest crystal—
She was like the sun making red in her rising
The clouds of dawn with the flame of her light.

JUDAH HALEVI
(*Translated by Nina Salaman*)

LOVE SONGS

I The Splendor of Thine Eyes

Come, Ophra, fill my cup—but not with wine,
The splendor of thine eyes therein let shine;
So shall the draught thou pour'st this night in Spain,
Bear to far lands and days, thy fame—and mine!

II The Hot Flame of My Grief

Beautiful as the pomegranate is the white face of Ophra when she
    blushes;
And I, that must part from her, weep—
Until the hot flame of my grief dries up my tears.

III Why Should I Grieve?

Why should I grieve? The purling of the brook,
The throstle's song, I hear. On couch of blooms,
More brilliant than the weave of Persia's looms,
I lie beneath the myrtle's shade, and look
On the bright necklace of the turtle dove—
And dream—and dream, ah me, of my lost love.

IV Beautiful Is the Loved One

Beautiful is the loved one
As she sways in the dance
Like a bough of the myrtle,
Her unbound tresses billowing about her.
She slays me with the arrows of her glances—
They are drunk with my blood—
But she shows no mercy.

V   When She Plays upon the Harp or Lute

Beautiful are the fingers of the loved one;
When she plays upon the harp or lute,
They fly over the strings swiftly as arrows,
And smoothly as the pen of a ready writer.
When she lets the music of her voice be heard,
Throstle and robin upon the branches
Hush their song.

VI   Those Beauteous Maids

But give me for my soul, those beauteous maids,
With hair like night, with faces like the moon—
Singing, with lutes held to their breasts, they seem
Like nursing mothers, to their babes that croon.

MOSES IBN EZRA
(*Translated by Solomon Solis-Cohen*)

AWAKE, MY FAIR
(*To her sleeping love*)

Awake, my fair, my love, awake,
That I may gaze on thee!
And if one fain to kiss thy lips
Thou in thy dreams dost see,
Lo, I myself then of my dream
The interpreter will be.

JUDAH HALEVI
(*Translated by Alice Lucas*)

With Hopeless Love

With hopeless love my heart is sick,
Confession bursts my lips' restraint.
That thou, my love, dost cast me off,
Hath touched me with a death-like taint.

I view the land both near and far,
To me it seems a prison vast.
Throughout its breadth, where'er I look,
My eyes are met by doors locked fast.

And though the world stood open wide,
Though angel hosts filled ev'ry space,
To me 'twere destitute of charm
Didst thou withdraw thy face.

Strange Love

Perchance in days to come,
When men and all things change,
They'll marvel at my love,
And call it passing strange.

Without I seem most calm,
But fires rage within—
'Gainst me as none before,
Thou didst a grievous sin.

What! tell the world my woe!
That were exceeding vain.
With mocking smile they'd say,
"You know, he is not sane!"

Elegy
(On the death of the woman he loved)

In pain she bore the son who her embrace
Would never know. Relentless death spread straight
His nets for her, and she, scarce animate,
Unto her husband signed: I ask this grace,
My friend, let not harsh death our love efface;
To our babes, its pledges, dedicate
Thy faithful care; for vainly they await
A mother's smile each childish fear to chase.
And to my uncle, prithee, write. Deep pain
I brought his heart. Consumed by love's regret
He roved, a stranger in his home. I fain
Would have him shed a tear, nor love forget.
He seeketh consolation's cup, but first
His soul with bitterness must quench its thirst.

My Love Is Like a Myrtle

My love is like a myrtle tree,
When at the dance her hair falls down.
Her eyes deal death most pitiless,
Yet who would dare on her to frown?

Said I to sweetheart: "Why dost thou resent
The homage to thy grace by old men paid?"
She answered me with question pertinent:
"Dost thou prefer a widow to a maid?"

MOSES IBN EZRA
(Translated by Solomon Solis-Cohen)

I AM MY BELOVED'S

I am my beloved's,
And his desire is toward me.
Come, my beloved, let us go forth into the field;
Let us lodge in the villages.
Let us get up early to the vineyards;
Let us see whether the vine hath budded,
Whether the vine-blossom be opened,
And the pomegranates be in flower;
There will I give thee my love.
The mandrakes give forth fragrance,
And at our doors are all manner of precious fruits,
New and old,
Which I have laid up for thee, O my beloved.

SONG OF SONGS 1:11–14

COME, LET US EXULT IN LOVE'S PASSION

Come, let us exult in love's passion!
Beloved, let's shout, let us sing,
As long as dark clouds have not gathered
And smiles grace the skies of our spring;

As long as our cheeks are yet flaming,
And tremulous hearts loudly beat;
While gladness and youth yet abide there,
Though ready to sound their retreat.

As long as the shades have not fallen,
Till Death to his dungeon us bring,
Come, let us exult in love's passion!
Beloved, let's shout, let us sing!

SAUL TCHERNIKHOVSKY
(*Translated by Harry H. Fein*)

A WOMAN OF VALOUR

A woman of valour who can find?
For her price is far above rubies.
The heart of her husband doth safely trust in her,
And he hath no lack of gain.
She doeth him good and not evil
All the days of her life.
She seeketh wool and flax,
And worketh willingly with her hands.
She is like the merchant ships;
She bringeth her food from afar.
She riseth also while it is yet night,
And giveth food to her household,
And a portion to her maidens.
She considereth a field, and buyeth it;
With the fruit of her hands she planteth a vineyard.
She girdeth her loins with strength,
And maketh strong her arms.
She perceiveth that her merchandise is good;
Her lamp goeth not out by night.
She layeth her hands to the distaff,
And her hands hold the spindle.
She stretcheth out her hand to the poor;
Yea, she reacheth forth her hands to the needy.
She is not afraid of the snow for her household;
For all her household are clothed with scarlet.
She maketh for herself coverlets;
Her clothing is fine linen and purple.
Her husband is known in the gates,
When he sitteth among the elders of the land.
She maketh linen garments and selleth them;
And delivereth girdles unto the merchant.
Strength and dignity are her clothing;
And she laugheth at the time to come.
She openeth her mouth with wisdom;
And the law of kindness is on her tongue.
She looketh well to the ways of her household,
And eateth not the bread of idleness.

Her children rise up, and call her blessed;
Her husband also, and he praiseth her:
'Many daughters have done valiantly,
But thou excellest them all.'
Grace is deceitful, and beauty is vain;
But a woman that feareth the Lord, she shall be praised.
Give her the fruit of her hands;
And let her works praise her in the gates.

PROVERBS 31:10–31

LONELINESS

Could I meet one who understood all . . .
Without word, without search,
Confession or lie,
Without asking why.

I would spread before him, like a white cloth,
The heart and the soul . . .
The filth and the gold.
Perceptive, he would understand.

And after I had plundered the heart,
When all had been emptied and given away,
I would feel neither anguish nor pain,
But would know how rich I became.

HANNAH SENESH
(*Translated by Ruth Finer Mintz*)

Whence and whither
We had no inkling,
But the eyes that saw her,
She set them twinkling.

From an unknown country,
Some land far away
She came like a bird
Laughing and gay.

Lightsome and lively,
She went up and down
And set in commotion
The whole of our town.

The slips and byways,
The greenwood path,
Rang with her singing
And echoed her laugh.

That day or that night
As she walked in the street
The youth of our town
Fell flat at her feet.

That day or that night,
In every house,
A bickering started
'Twixt man and his spouse.

Good women whispered
O'er knitting pins,
Old men winked slyly,
And scratched their chins.

Father and mother
Slept not at night,
For their daughter's bridegroom
Was out of sight.

Then one day she vanished
Without a "goodbye!"
No one knew whither
And no one knew why.

Swift as a bird
Flies from a tree:
No one foresaw it,
Nor dreamt it could be.

The laughter was hushed,
The wood was neglected:
There was no one in it.
And no one expected.

As on dull grey days
That come out of season,
All went depressed
Without knowing the reason.

The boys came home punctual,
All meek and mild,
Bride and bridegroom
Were reconciled.

Young husbands sit
And yawn with their wives,
Who were never so loving
In all their lives.

No fun in the dark,
In the lane no delight—
Father and mother
Can sleep all night.

No quarrels, no shouts,
And nothing unlawful,
Peace in and peace out—
And the dullness is awful!

CHAIM NACHMAN BIALIK
(*Translated by Helena Frank*)

EVE

I love Adam. He is brave of heart,
his blood is generous; and he, like God,
is wise. But the serpent whispers things
that are so strange. They hurt—and they caress.

When Adam sleeps, Eden lies desolate;
its birds are silent and its grass is wet.
And then *he* kindles, calling from the thicket,
a bonfire in my heart. "Pick it! Pick it!"

How good to feel at dawn Adam's warm hand
caress my flesh again, and in the hush
listen to the coursing of its blood.
But every bush of day that drinks the light
bends to a darkness. Eden is enchanted
only till night awakes the shadow in the brush.

YAACOV FICHMAN
(*Translated by Robert Friend*)

WITHIN MY HEART

Within my heart I held concealed
My love so tender and so true;
But overflowing tears revealed
What I would fain have hid from view.
My heart could evermore repress
The woe that tell-tale tears confess.

JUDAH AL-HARIZI
(*Translated by Emma Lazarus*)

THE MAIDEN

She spun in silence a red thread,
Red as a pomegranate's heart.
The king inside his chamber said:
"She spins me clothes to wear at court."

She spun in silence a black thread,
That darkens day. Far from the king,
The thief locked up in prison said:
"She spins me clothes in which to hang."

She spun in silence a gold thread,
A sword of lightning. On his way,
The harlequin pranced past and said:
"She spins me clothes in which to play."

She spun in silence a grey thread,
The ancestor all colors keep.
The beggar to his mongrel said:
"She spins me clothes in which to weep."

She rose, the colored threads she took,
And wove them all into a mesh,
And then she went to the brook,
And there she washed her perfect flesh.

And she put on the woven thing,
And was made beautiful forever:
And she since then is thief and king,
And harlequin and beggar.

NATAN ALTERMAN
(*Translated by Dom Moraes*)

LOVE SONG

The long-closed door, oh open it again,
   send me back once more my fawn that had fled.
On the day of our reunion, thou shalt rest by my side,
   there wilt thou shed over me the streams of thy delicious perfume.
Oh, beautiful bride, what is the form of thy friend, that thou
   say to me, Release him, send him away?
He is the beautiful-eyed one of ruddy glorious aspect—that is
   my friend, him do thou detain.
Hail to thee, Son of my friend, the ruddy, the bright-colored one!
Hail to thee whose temples are like a pomegranate.
Hasten to the refuge of thy sister, and protect the son of Isaiah
   against the troops of the Ammonites.
What art thou, O Beauty, that thou shouldst inspire love? that thy
   voice should ring like the voices of the bells upon the priestly garments?
The hour wherein thou desireth my love, I shall hasten to meet thee.
Softly will I drop thee like the dew upon Hermon.

JUDAH AL-HARIZI
(*Translated by Emma Lazarus*)

OPHRA

Ophra washeth her garments in the waters
Of my tears, and spreadeth them out in the sunshine of her radiance.
She demandeth no water of the fountains, having my two eyes;
And no other sunshine than her beauty.

JUDAH HALEVI
(*Translated by Nina Salaman*)

TO THE BRIDEGROOM

Rejoice, O young man, in thy youth,
And gather the fruit thy joy shall bear,
Thou and the wife of thy youth,
Turning now to thy dwelling to enter there.

Glorious blessings of God, who is One,
Shall come united upon thine head;
Thine house shall be at peace from dread,
Thy foes' uprising be undone.
Thou shalt lay thee down in a safe retreat;
Thou shalt rest, and thy sleep be sweet.

In thine honor, my bridegroom, prosper and live;
Let thy beauty arise and shine forth fierce;
And the heart of thine enemies God shall pierce,
And the sins of thy youth will He forgive,
And bless thee in increase and all thou shalt do,
When thou settest thine hand thereto.

And remember the Rock, Creator of thee,
When the goodness cometh which He shall bring;
For sons out of many days shall spring,
And even as thy days thy strength shall be.
Blessed be thou when thou enterest,
And thy going out shall be blest.

'Mid the perfect and wise shall thy portion lie,
So thou be discreet where thou turnest thee;
And thine house shall be builded immovably,
And "Peace" thou shalt call, and God shall reply;
And peace shall be thine abode; and sealed
Thy bond with the stones of the field.

Thy glory shall rise, nor make delay;
And thee shall He call and choose; and thy light
In the gloom, in the darkness of night,
Then shall break forth like the darkness of day;
And out from the shining light of the morn
Shall the dew of thy youth be born.

JUDAH HALEVI
(*Translated by Nina Salaman*)

IF NIGHT NEARS YOUR WINDOW

If night nears your window
In nakedness come out to him.

He'll ripple softly, he'll darken
Round your still beauty,
Touching the tip of your breasts.

I'll stand, a lost traveller, with him,
And quietly we'll both feel desire.
Come to us, who are both darkling:

Your two eyes shall travel before
Us, to light
The way for me and my friend.

DAVID FOGEL
(*Translated by Dom Moraes*)

NOTE: Thérèse du Meun was a woman of the French aristocracy who lived at the end of the sixteenth century in the environs of Avignon, in Provence. When she was about forty years old, she fell in love with a young Italian who was tutoring her sons, and dedicated to him forty-one sonnets. When the young Italian left her house, she burned all her poems and sought the seclusion of a nunnery. The memory of her poems remained only as a legend transmitted by her contemporaries.

—LEAH GOLDBERG

(EDITOR'S NOTE: The following two sonnets are taken from the twelve which Leah Goldberg "reconstructed," as it were, from the above-mentioned poems, irretrievably lost.)

Sonnet III

If you discarded me, expelled me far
Into the wilderness, a prey to sorrow,
To death, starvation, loneliness and horror,
As Abraham drove his concubine, Hagar—

If callously you let my heartblood drip,
If like a slut you had me grieved, insulted,
Not thus would my hurt feelings have revolted,
Nor my defiance be so bitter, crisp.

But you regard me as a highborn dame,
An inaccessible, exalted lady,
You hardly dare even pronounce my name.

A lofty castle, fortified and blocked.
With fear of shame my steps are stilted, shady,
My fists are hammering against the rock.

Sonnet VIII

The raindrop filaments, like strings, close tight
Upon the window-pane. My friend, please kindle
The hearth-fire. Let us sit among the lights
And watch the silhouettes between us dwindle.

How well you fit into the greyish guise
Of rainy days. Your youthfulness is caught then
Against a double light of flame and autumn—
My heart the ardour and my mind the ice.

How much I relish this delicious fraud:
To hide my passion in maternal rolls
Of prudent care, yet leave the spell unbroken.

Nor will your brow be clouded by the thought
That here, right here before the glowing coals,
An hour of love I pilfered as a token.

LEAH GOLDBERG
(*Translated by Abraham Birman*)

THE ELUSIVE MAID

Thrice-cruel maid, may Heaven frown on thee,
For that by day thou hidest thyself from me,
And yet thou robbest me of my nightly rest,
For that thy face is in my eyes impressed.

ABRAHAM IBN CHASDAI
(*Translated by J. Chotzner*)

THERE WAS A KING IN JUDAH

There was a king in Judah,
The elders king him crowned;
His sword he bravely wielded
Upon a lofty mound.
There was a king in Judah
Upon a lofty mound.

There was a king in Judah,
Of many maids possessed.
They plied the humming spindle;
He loved the comeliest.
There was a king in Judah,
He loved the comeliest.

She made no use of ointments,
Nor myrrh's extravagance;
For love the maid was fashioned,
Her eyes shed radiance.
She made no use of ointments,
Her eyes shed radiance.

There was a king in Judah,
The hills housed Hittites then.
He armed his trained servants,
And he led to war his men.
There was a king in Judah,
And he led to war his men.

While on the slope, forgot he
All wealth that he did own,
His treasures greatly lauded,
His palace widely known.
While on the slope, forgot he
His palace widely known.

A dart whizzed by . . . he marked not,
The danger he did brave,
But one, but one beheld he,
To radiant eyes a slave.
A dart whizzed by . . . he marked not,
To radiant eyes a slave.

He knew he'd ne'er return
From the path whereon he trod.
Enchanted by the maiden,
He died for Love, his god.
He knew he'd ne'er return.
He died for Love, his god.

SAUL TCHERNIKHOVSKY
(*Translated by Harry H. Fein*)

HAPPINESS AMIDST TROUBLES

Whenever troublous hours I find
That rob me of my peace of mind,
To thee I haste, my little bride,
And all forget, when by thy side.

Let others load their castled towers,
Their magic grots, their gladsome bowers;
For me that place hath chiefest charms,
That brings me, dearest, to thine arms.

IMMANUEL DI ROMA
(*Translated by J. Chotzner*)

"Thy breath is far sweeter than honey,
Thy radiance brightens the day;
Thy voice is e'en softer than lyre-note,
Yet hear I its echoes alway.
Thy wit is as pure as thy witchery,
And both in thy face are displayed;
Alas! mid the maze of thy pleasaunce,
From the path to thy heart I have strayed."

Soft on my couch sleeping, dreaming,
I heard this, my lover's fond word;
Blushing a blush of new rapture,
Methought that I whispered, "My lord!
If thou canst desire my poor beauty
Stand not outside or afar;
Come, I will lead to thy garden,
For thine all my pleasaunces are."

"Beloved, thy words of allurement,
Like dew-drops refreshen my heart.
My soul boundeth free from its fetters,
My life leaves its longing and smart.
Come yield now thy lips to thy lover,
Come yield me the sweets of thy heart."

ABRAHAM IBN EZRA
(*Translated by Israel Abrahams*)

~ 43 ~

The Mirror

Into my eyes he loving looked,
My arms about his neck were twined,
And in the mirror of my eyes,
What but his image did he find?

Upon my dark-hued eyes he pressed
His lips with breath of passion rare.
The rogue! 'Twas not my eyes he kissed;
He kissed his picture mirrored there.

He Cometh

He cometh, O bliss!
Fly swiftly, ye winds,
Ye odorous breezes,
And tell him how long
I've waited for this!

O happy that night,
When sunk on thy breast,
Thy kisses fast falling,
And drunken with love,
My troth I did plight.

Again my sweet friend
Embraceth me close.
Yes, heaven doth bless us,
And now thou hast won
My love without end.

My Sweetheart's Dainty Lips

My sweetheart's dainty lips are red,
With ruby's crimson overspread;
Her teeth are like a string of pearls;
Adown her neck her clust'ring curls
In ebon hue vie with the night,
And o'er her features dances light.

The twinkling stars enthroned above
Are sisters to my dearest love.
We men should count it joy complete
To lay our service at her feet.
But ah! what rapture in her kiss!
A forecast 'tis of heav'nly bliss!

JUDAH HALEVI
(*Translated by Emma Lazarus*)

STRANGE MATRIMONY

My friend of twenty summers takes to bride
A maid of four score years of proud endeavour.
Some difference in their age be descried,
In their stupendous folly none whatever.

ISAAC BENJACOB
(*Translated by J. Chotzner*)

ODE TO A BRIDEGROOM

Rejoice, O bridegroom, in the wife of thy youth, thy comrade!
Let thy heart be merry now, and when thou shalt grow old
Sons to thy sons shalt thou see, thine old age's crown;
Sons who shall prosper and work in place of their pious sires.
Thy days in good shall be spent, thy years in pleasantness.
Floweth thy peace as a stream, riseth thy worth as its waves,
For peace shall be found in thy home, rest shall abide in thy dwelling.
Blessed be each day's work, blessed be thine all,
And thy bliss this assembly shall share, happy in thee.
By grace of us all ascend, thou and thy goodly company;
Rise we, too, to our feet, lovingly to greet thee;
One hope is now in all hearts, one prayer we utter,
Blessed be thy coming in, blessed be thy going forth.

UNKNOWN MEDIEVAL POET
(*Translated by Israel Abrahams*)

A HUSBAND'S COMPLAINT

By heaven's favour, I possess
Two treasures dearer far than gold;
A wife and cellar; I confess
The wine is young, the woman's old.
And nought could now my joy enhance
The crowd of mortal men among,
Unless it happened that, perchance,
The wine were old, the woman young.

SOLOMON MANDELKERN
(*Translated by J. Chotzner*)

A FATHER'S WEDDING POEM TO HIS SON

(From the "Silver Bowl")

My son, on this thy wedding day rejoice,
To song of mirth attune thy heart and voice.
Take thou the graceful doe, the royal bride,
With her thy joy and happiness divide.
A comely form, my darling son, is thine;
Corrupt it not, for 'tis a gift divine.
If thou wouldst see the gates of Paradise,
Refrain! Thy work on earth will thee suffice.
Yea, many rushing heaven's height to scale
In fruitless quests their life misspent bewail.
Behold reveal'd creation's mystery,
List to the strains of heaven's symphony;
And when the day of good report is nigh
E'en as Elijah thou shalt rise on high.
Three crowns there are, and these the world may love;
A blameless name is more, all crowns above.
Humbly pray God may crown thee with His Light,
To live 'mid men, with heart, with soul, with might.
Rejoice with her, thy graceful tender dove;
God bless you twain, with love as angels love.

> JOSEPH EZOBI
> *(Translated by D. I. Freedman)*

SONG TO THE WIFE OF HIS YOUTH

Not all is vanity, dear,
not all is pride and folly.
I scattered my days to the winds,
I broke my pact with money.
Only you I pursued, my dear,
Like the neck pursues the hangsman.

For you donned your kerchief, dear,
and you asked me to behold you.
And I swore not to taste my bread
till teeth rotted with your unripeness.
I swore to look at you, dear,
till my eyes grew dim with looking.

And sickness struck, my dear,
poverty covered our faces.
And sickness I called "my house,"
and poverty, "our daughter."
We were wretched as dogs, my dear,
and dogs fled from our presence.

Then iron appeared, my dear,
beheading me of you
And nothing remained except
my ashes pursuing your shoes.
For iron breaks, my dear,
but my thirst for you is unquenched.

The spirit hath no end, my dear;
the body has—and shatters.
Joy did not visit my house
and earth made me a pallet.
But the day you rejoice, my dear,
my dead eyes will rejoice in the darkness.

A day of joy, my dear,
will come and we will share it,
and you'll fall to the earth of my pact
when a coffin rope drops you to me.
Not all is vanity, dear,
not all is pride and folly.

NATAN ALTERMAN
(*Translated by Robert Friend*)

HIS WIFE

She turns and calls him by name
With the voice of every day.
How can I trust my voice
Not to give me away?

In the street, in the full light of day,
She walks by his side.
I in the dark of night
Must hide.

Bright and serene on her hand
Is her ring of gold.
The iron fetters I wear
Are stronger, seven fold.

RACHEL
(*Translated by Robert Friend*)

LOVE SONG

"See'st thou o'er my shoulder falling,
Snake-like ringlets waving free?
Have no fear, for they are twisted
To allure thee unto me."

Thus she spake, the gentle dove,
Listen to thy plighted love:
"Ah, how long I wait, until
Sweetheart cometh back (she said)
Laying his caressing hand
Underneath my burning head."

JUDAH HALEVI
(Translated by Emma Lazarus)

FOR A GIRL'S TRESSES

For a girl's tresses God burns in longing
And is not ashamed.
He has left the hermit's haven,
And strains for the breadths of scarlet—
Will you lust like a man, O God! . . .
You gleam like a male—
You have been as bad as I, a man!
Let me hound you now,
For you have hounded me,
Eternal God, O love! . . .

I. Z. RIMON
(Translated by Richard Flantz)

IF HE RETURNS

If he returns—he'll lift me into his car
That flies up blazing and high,
And he'll bring me his warm smiling breadth
And the calm blue distance in his eye.

From sights that were lost in the flames,
That paced through the storm's dreadful slings
Among pieces of serpents and stones,
And animals, faces and wings—

Not a word will I be able to say,
Not a thing will I be able to show
Of his height that keeps rising higher,
Of his good and gentle glow,

My glance will ripen like bread,
My face will rise like a fruit.
For he's brought me,
He's brought me to tears,
In a daily holiness to brood.

I shall break my crust into two
And wait on my stoop, hand on knee,
They will come:
The wanderer, the blue—
To drink my water with me.

YOCHEVED BAT-MIRIAM
(*Translated by Richard Flantz*)

REJOICE, O YOUTH, IN THE LOVELY HIND
(Fragment from the Wedding Song honoring Rabbi Solomon Ben Matir)

Rejoice, O youth, in the lovely hind,
And sing ye both in ecstasy of joy.
Delight thou, O bridegroom, in a figure graceful as the palm,
And lissom as the branches of the myrtle;
Fear not, at twilight, the tinkling of her neck-chains
Or the rustling of her headdress;
Nor quail before the dove-like eyes,
Drunk with the wine of passion.
Let thy heart be firm in the embrace of arms
Adorned with bracelets and brave with bangles,
And flee not from the snake-like locks
That coil about a face bathed in maiden blushes;
Verily, they come to meet thee in peace,
Thou they veil and hide from thee the splendor of her countenance.
And the pomegranates in the garden of lilies,
Behold, with studs of clove are they fastened;
Let thy hand stroke them softly,
Be thou tender in thy caresses.
And know that time is the servant of thy will,
That the hours are assembled to do thy wish;
They hasten to bring near thy desires,
And all that vexes thy heart will they put to flight.

MOSES IBN EZRA
(*Translated by Solomon Solis-Cohen*)

MARRIAGE SONG

Fair is my dove, my loved one,
None can with her compare:
Yea, comely as Jerusalem,
Like unto Tirzah fair.

Shall she in tents unstable
A wanderer abide,
While in my heart awaits her
A dwelling deep and wide?

The magic of her beauty
Has stolen my heart away:
Not Egypt's wise enchanters
Held half such wondrous sway.

E'en as the changing opal
In varying lustre glows,
Her face at every moment
New charms and sweetness shows.

White lilies and red roses
There blossom on one stem:
Her lips of crimson berries
Tempt mine to gather them.

By dusky tresses shaded
Her brow gleams fair and pale,
Like to the sun at twilight,
Behind a cloudy veil.

Her beauty shames the day-star,
And makes the darkness light:
Day in her radiant presence
Grows seven times more bright.

This is a lonely lover!
Come, fair one, to his side,
That happy be together
The bridegroom and the bride!

The hour of love approaches
That shall make one of twain:
Soon may be thus united
All Israel's hosts again!

JUDAH HALEVI
(*Translated by Alice Lucas*)

A STAR THERE FELL

A star there fell, a star there sank
In darkness, in the deep of night—
Although it sank, it mattered not,
For countless stars still shed their light.

A tear is trickling from my eye,
And toward thee the tear does flow—
Thou canst not see, for countless tears
Are ever streaming here below.

ZALMAN SCHNEOUR
(*Translated by Harry H. Fein*)

Behold, thou art fair, my love; behold, thou art fair;
Thine eyes are as doves behind thy veil;
Thy hair is as a flock of goats,
That trail down from mount Gilead.
Thy teeth are like a flock of ewes all shaped alike,
Which are come up from the washing;
Whereof all are paired,
And none faileth among them.
Thy lips are like a thread of scarlet,
And thy mouth is comely;
Thy temples are like a pomegranate split open
Behind thy veil.
Thy neck is like the tower of David
Builded with turrets,
Whereon there hang a thousand shields,
All the armour of the mighty men.
Thy two breasts are like two fawns
That are twins of a gazelle,
Which feed among the lilies.
Until the day break,
And the shadows flee away,
I will get me to the mountain of myrrh,
And to the hill of frankincense.
Thou art all fair, my love;
And there is no spot in thee.

SONG OF SONGS *4:1–7*

THE MARRIAGE JESTER'S SONG

Hurrah hurrah, let us all be glad
Now that the bridegroom has come to Brod.

Up wi' you players, and take your tools,
Fiddle and don't stand there like fools.

Start up a tune and bang the drum
Now that the bridegroom to town has come.

Shout aloud, burst into song,
And the whole town will come and dance in the throng.

And you my brethren without a care,
Clap your hands to honor the pair.

Beloved and pleasant as in tales of yore,
Mistress Pessele and Reb Sheftel Shor,

And in honor of his father by all men discerned,
Our wealthy Master Reb Vovi the learned,

And in honor of the father known to us each one,
Namely the Hassid Reb Yudel Nathanson,

And in honor of their wives whose names I don't know,
And of families and those who have come for the show

From all the world over, from Brod and Rohatin
May they enjoy themselves for ever with their kin.

S. Y. AGNON
(*Translated by I. M. Lask*)

Father's gone far, far away
And taken with some cash,
Gone to a place where lads learn Torah
For to find his girl her match.

Master Rabbi, head of the school,
Money, thank God, I do not lack.
I've come here to fetch my daughter
A scholar bridegroom back.

Answers the head o' the school and says,
There are three such as you desire,
One a prodigy, one ever studying—
The third is a flame of fire.

You'll find none better in any school
Or any town or land.
Happy the man who'll choose one for
To take his daughter's hand.

Father answers and says to him,
Three maids, Master, have I, have I.
Answers the head o' the school and says,
Then seize ere others do try.

These sprigs o' the Torah lush with knowledge,
Lads better far than the best.
Father's gone far, far away,
To bring us scholar bridegrooms blest.

S. Y. AGNON
(*Translated by I. M. Lask*)

WINGED ITS WAY TO ME
HER LETTER

Winged its way to me her letter,
And therein these words were written:
"All my soul hath loved and cherished,
All my spirit ever fostered,
Yea, the well-spring of my being,
And my faith and aspiration—
Was this but, friend of my bosom,
Spring of life, Oh soul of my soul,
Was this but a dream fast fleeting?

"Hast forgotten? Nay, thou canst not!
Nay, thou dar'st not have forgotten
What one breath of life hath planted,
Planted in our inmost being;
What one glowing sun hath lighted
In the heavens o'er us spreading;
What one golden dream hath poured out
Over our united spirit—
Nay, thou wilt not dare, nay, never,
From our heart to pluck the flower,
Which God's hand divine hath planted—"

Yet again I read the letter,
And a gentle hand and tender
Seems to carve upon the tablet
Of my heart, those sorrow-laden
Words: "Thou wilt not dare, nay, never,
From our heart to pluck the flower,
Which God's hand divine hath planted."

And from out the golden sunshine
Streaming through my open window,
Once again doth rise before me
Radiant her loved image;
She it is in all her beauty:

Light as on the wind's wings hov'ring,
As a butterfly bright sparkling,
Wholly light and child of sunshine,
As of light for light created—
And behold, those sweet eyes shining,
Twin doves they and full of silence,
And from out the pupils, softly
Shines the light of peace and quiet,
Light of purity and kindness—
In the gold of radiant sunshine
Now appear her eyes before me,
With a mute rebuke o'ershadowed,
And they smite my heart with anguish;
Softly gazing do they ask me:
"Was it, love, ah tell me truly,
But a dream and false enchantment?"

Nay, beloved! I have loved thee,
And I love thee yet as ever;
Even when I left thee, dearest—
It was for the love I bore thee:
Too pure thou to be my friend, yea,
and too holy to be with me;
Be thou God and angel to me,
Pray to thee will I and serve thee;
May thy memory be sacred;
Shine to me in the bright sunlight,
Beckon from the starry heavens,
Call to me from my heart's beating,
Tremble in my burning teardrop—
God created me to serve thee!
Tears I shed and sighs I utter,
And my breath and my heart's throbbing,
Yea, the last dream of my slumbers—
These, my offerings I bring thee,
Till life's gates are closed upon me.

CHAIM NACHMAN BIALIK
(*Translated by Bertha Beinkinstadt*)

AFTERNOON LIGHT

Drink deep, my heart, of brightest noon,
But trust not its tranquility!
Quietly, in the blue light, lurk
Mourning winds one cannot see.

Treacherous is the afternoon rest.
Do not trust it when it comes.
A bright canopy is woven slowly
By a hidden hand over horror's depths.

Dreams of purest white
Dig, for something, a grave:
You awake—their song stills:
Their gold tarnishes, their light pales.

Do not believe in the light of afternoon
Nor in its deceiving rest.
Sure is one hour, one hour alone,
Faithful in its distress.

This is the muted evening hour—
Lingering away in the day's edge.
It will not fail, believe in it.
Walk erect to meet it.
In the light of day, in the golden white
That it come, my heart, await!

YAACOV FICHMAN
(*Translated by Ruth Finer Mintz*)

SHELTER ME BENEATH YOUR PINION

Shelter me beneath your pinion
With a mother's, sister's care,
And your lap shall be my refuge
And my nest of stifled prayer.

And when tenderness of twilight
Falls, my pain shall give a sign:
There is youth, they say, to squander—
Where is mine?

And another secret longing
Burns my spirit like a flame:
There is love, they say, to garner—
Love? What is that name?

By the stars my life was pilfered,
By a dream that died, and see—
Naked now, and empty-handed—
What is left for me?

Shelter me beneath your pinion
With a mother's, sister's care,
And your lap shall be my refuge
And my nest of stifled prayer.

CHAIM NACHMAN BIALIK
(*Translated by Maurice Samuel*)

I sleep, but my heart waketh;
Hark! my beloved knocketh:
"Open to me, my sister, my love, my undefiled;
For my head is filled with dew,
My locks with the drops of the night."
I have put off my coat;
How shall I put it on?
I have washed my feet;
How shall I defile them?
My beloved put in his hand by the hole of the door,
And my heart was moved for him.
I rose up to open to my beloved;
And my hands dropped with myrrh,
And my fingers with flowing myrrh,
Upon the handles of the bar.
I opened to my beloved;
But my beloved had turned away, and was gone.
My soul failed me when he spoke.
I sought him, but I could not find him.
I called him, but he gave me no answer.
The watchmen that go about the city found me,
They smote me, they wounded me;
The keepers of the wall took away my mantle from me.
"I adjure you, O daughters of Jerusalem,
If ye find my beloved,
What will ye tell him?
That I am love-sick."
"What is thy beloved more than another beloved,
O thou fairest among women?
What is thy beloved more than another beloved,
That thou dost so adjure us?"
"My beloved is white and ruddy,
Pre-eminent above ten thousand.

His head is as the most fine gold,
His locks are curled,
And black as a raven.
His eyes are like doves
Beside the water-brooks;
Washed with milk,
And fitly set.
His cheeks are as a bed of spices,
As banks of sweet herbs;
His lips are as lilies,
Dropping with flowing myrrh.
His hands are as rods of gold
Set with beryl;
His body is as polished ivory
Overlaid with sapphires.
His legs are as pillars of marble,
Set upon sockets of fine gold;
His aspect is like Lebanon,
Excellent as the cedars.
His mouth is most sweet;
Yea, he is altogether lovely.
This is my beloved, and this is my friend,
O daughters of Jerusalem."
"Whither is thy beloved gone,
O thou fairest among women?
Whither hath thy beloved turned him,
That we may seek him with thee?"
"My beloved has gone down to his garden,
To the beds of spices,
To feed in the gardens,
And to gather lilies.
I am my beloved's, and my beloved is mine,
That feedeth among the lilies."

SONG OF SONGS 5:2–16; 6:1–3

ONE TWO THREE

One two three four five six seven eight
Marry your girl before it's too late.

Do not reflect, do not delay,
Or someone else will snatch her away.

Once I had honey, but did not eat,
And another came and found it sweet.

There were two sisters—one was fair,
The second was dark, and dark her hair.

They were both lovely and good to see,
And I loved them both equally.

I pondered and pondered with aching head.
I couldn't decide which to wed.

Months passed and still I could not see
Which I should ask my wife to be.

Till alas two devils came one day,
And carried both of them away.

Now I am old and sick and worn,
Broken-hearted and forlorn.

And I say to all who will listen to me,
Don't let your lives like my life be.

One two three four five six seven eight
Marry your girl before it's too late.

Do not reflect, do not delay.
Don't let another snatch her away.

CHAIM NACHMAN BIALIK
(*Translated by Joseph Leftwich*)

TIRZAH

Day after day as the day sets,
   And the sun's heating is waning,
There walks Tirzah, lonely faun,
   Into the garden singing.

Day after day as day sets—
   To listen to her singing,
A cherub descends from the skies
   To the garden winging.

In mysterious quiet all is wrapped,
   The shadow spreading thickens—
And Tirzah singing, still sings on,
   And still the cherub listens.

Then as a sudden tremor moves
   Through leaves of tree about her,
Tirzah a slight moment shudders,
   Stares expectantly behind her.

But nothing whatever does she see,
   Completely unaware,
Confident she sings again
   For the cherub's listening ear.

YAACOV COHEN
(*Translated by Ruth Finer Mintz*)

NEITHER DAILY NEITHER NIGHTLY

("Lo Bayom ve'lo Balayla"—a folk song)

Neither daily neither nightly
Through the fields I wander lightly.

Not in Europe nor in Asia
Out there stands an old acacia.

This acacia I importune:
Thorny One, do tell me my fortune.

Answer me and do not tarry—
Who's the one I'm gonna marry?

From the highland or the lowland?
Lithuania or Poland?

Is he rich, equipped with carriage,
Or the poorest of the parish?

And a brooch, a little trinket,
Or a necklace, will he bring it?

His hair, is it thin or rippling?
Is he widowed or a stripling?

Or an old man? Then I'd rather
Die, and so I'll tell my father:

"Though my thread of life you sever
I shan't take an old man—never!"

I'll shriek like a wounded starling,
"Not a greybeard, Poppa darling!"

CHAIM NACHMAN BIALIK
(Translated by Abraham Birman)

~ 69 ~

ONE SUMMER EVENING

They weave, the daughters of the star-crowned night,
A weft of silvery shine,
And clothe alike the sanctified high priest
And him who herds the swine.

One summer eve, when everyone is out
And no one in,
A man went forth, full of his big desires
His little sins to sin.

Impatient, eager-eyed, one prayer had he
In his heart aglow;
O virtuous stars, make haste, come out of heaven—
Harlots, come out below!

Light, wanton music from the garden comes
Floating on the breeze;
A wisp of veil, a scarf, an apron-gleam
Among the trees.

Like traders of desire the stars wink down,
Their golden eyelids goad;
And passion stirs even in blades of grass,
In stones beside the road.

Up from the river, down from balconies,
There comes a shout
Of laughter, then—a window-curtain falling,
The lights put out.

Hush, flesh commands, the whole world gluts and quaffs
With its own vintage drunken.
He rolls, demented, in his spew, and wallows
In fleshly pleasure sunken.

They weave, the daughters of the star-crowned night
A weft of silvery shine!
And clothe alike the sanctified high priest
And him who herds the swine.

CHAIM NACHMAN BIALIK
(*Translated by Helena Frank*)

I H A V E L E A R N E D T O M O U L D

I have learned to mould and sculpt in matter,
And to pour the lights of the soul.
On the heights of mountain summits
Stands the princess,
Her body moulded in marble.
All glory gleams from her sculpted eyes,
Till grace dissolves in fainting.
The sun of Jerusalem shone on her . . .
Terribly did I burn and yearn for her,
And I long for her still . . .
And she called in her pride: "He who sings my song,
His shall I be! . . ."
Now I shall go, now I shall come, and say:
"I have learned your song, here it is in my mouth:
Your body is fairer than the marble of skies,
O daughter of kings,
And the radiance of your eyes than the radiance of souls;
With prayer and fasting have I discovered your secret—
Be mine! . . ."

I. Z. RIMON
(*Translated by Richard Flantz*)

Return, return, O Shulammite;
Return, return, that we may look upon thee.

What will ye see in the Shulammite?
As it were a dance of two companies.

How beautiful are thy steps in sandals,
O prince's daughter!
The roundings of thy thighs are like the links of a chain,
The work of the hands of a skilled workman.
Thy navel is like a round goblet,
Wherein no mingled wine is wanting;
Thy belly is like a heap of wheat
Set about with lilies.
Thy two breasts are like two fawns
That are twins of a gazelle.
Thy neck is as a tower of ivory;
Thine eyes as the pools in Heshbon,
By the gate of Bath-rabbim;
Thy nose is like the tower of Lebanon
Which looketh toward Damascus.
Thy head upon thee is like Carmel,
And the hair of thy head like purple;
The king is held captive in the tresses thereof.
How fair and how pleasant art thou,
O love, for delights!
This thy stature is like to a palm-tree,
And thy breasts to clusters of grapes.
I said: "I will climb up into the palm-tree,
I will take hold of the branches thereof;
And let thy breasts be as clusters of the vine,
And the smell of thy countenance like apples;
And the roof of thy mouth like the best wine,
That glideth down smoothly for my beloved,
Moving gently the lips of those that are asleep."

SONG OF SONGS 7:1–10

~ 73 ~

MY GARDEN

Two steps from my garden rail
Sleeps my well beneath its pail:
    Every Sabbath comes my love
    And I let him drink thereof.

All the world is sleeping now
Like the fruit beneath the bough.
    Father, mother, both are gone
    And my heart wakes here alone.

And the pail awakes with me,
Dripping, dripping, drowsily:
    Drops of gold and crystal clear . . .
    And my love is drawing near.

Hist! I think that something stirred;
Was it he, or but a bird?
    Dearest friend, my lover dear,
    There is no with me here.

By the trough we sit and speak,
Hand in hand and cheek to cheek;
    Hear this riddle: Can you tell
    Why the pitcher seeks the well?

That you cannot answer, nor
What the pail is weeping for?
    Morn to even, drop by drop,
    Fall its tears and cannot stop.

This then tell me, why my breast
Daylong, nightlong is oppressed.
    Spoke my mother truth in saying
    That your heart from me was straying?

And my lover answered: See,
Enemies have slandered me.
   Ere another year be gone,
   We shall marry, foolish one.

On that golden day of days
Shall the summer be ablaze.
   Fruited branches overhead
   Shall in benediction spread.

Friend and kinsman, young and old,
Shall be gathered to behold,
   And with music and with mirth
   They shall come to lead us forth.

And the bridal canopy
In this place shall lifted be.
   I shall slip a ring of gold
   On this finger that I hold,

And pronounce the blessing: "Thee
God makes consecrate to me,"
   And my enemies shall there
   Burst with envy and despair.

     CHAIM NACHMAN BIALIK
     (*Translated by Maurice Samuel*)

ON A HILL
(*From "Songs of the People"*)

On a hill there blooms a palm
'Twixt Tigris and Euphrates old,
And among the leafy branches
Sits the phoenix, bird of gold.

Bird of gold, go forth and find me
Him whose bride I am to be:
Search and circle till thou find him,
Bind him, bring him, bird, to me.

If thou hast no thread of scarlet,
Give him greeting without end:
Tell him, golden bird, my spirit
Languishes towards my friend.

Tell him: Now the garden blossoms,
Closed except to his command;
Mid the leaves the golden apple
Waits and trembles for his hand.

Tell him, nightly on my pillow
Wakes the longing without name,
And the whiteness of my body
Burns my couch as with a flame.

If he comes not, hear my secret:
All prepared my coffer stands;
Linen, silk, and twenty singlets
Wrought and knitted by these hands.

And the softest of all feathers
By my mother plucked and stored:
Through the nights she filled the cushions
For her daughter's bridal hoard.

And the bridal veil of silver
Waits to deck me when I marry:
Bride and dowry both are ready—
Wherefore does the bridegroom tarry?

✻

Seethe and whisper, magic potion:
Thus the phoenix makes reply:
"In the night to thy beloved
With my secret will I fly.

"In his dreams I give thy greeting,
In his dreams, reveal thy face:
Lo! Upon a broomstick mounted
Unto thee he flies apace.

"And he comes and speaks: 'Behold me,
Oh, my joy, my hope, my pride:
Not with golden gifts or dowry,
But with love become my bride.

"'Gold and silk I have aplenty—
Fire of youth and ringlets fine:
Both I give thee—swiftly, lightly,
Come to me, beloved mine.'"

✻

When the night was dark above me,
And the stars with clouds were stilled,
On his quest the phoenix vanished—
And his words are unfulfilled.

And at morn, at noon, at even,
Still I watch the clouds of fire:
"Clouds above me, answer, Wherefore
Comes he not, my heart's desire?"

CHAIM NACHMAN BIALIK
(*Translated by Maurice Samuel*)

THE DOVE

A dove of rarest worth
And sweet exceedingly;
Alas, why does she turn
And fly so far from me?
I my fond heart a tent,
Should aye prepared to be.
My poor heart she has caught
With magic spells and wiles.
I do not sigh for gold,
But for her mouth that smiles;
Her hue it is so bright,
She half makes blind my sight.

※

The day at last is here
Filled full of love's sweet fire;
The twain shall soon be one,
Shall stay their fond desire.
Ah! would my tribe should chance
On such deliverance!

JUDAH HALEVI
(*Translated by Amy Levy*)

LOVE

The rustle of each falling leaf,
The cooing of the gentle dove,
The roaring of the angry sea,
They each and all betoken—love.

SAMUELE ROMANELLI
(*Translated by A. B. Rhine*)

INDEX OF TITLES

INDEX OF AUTHORS